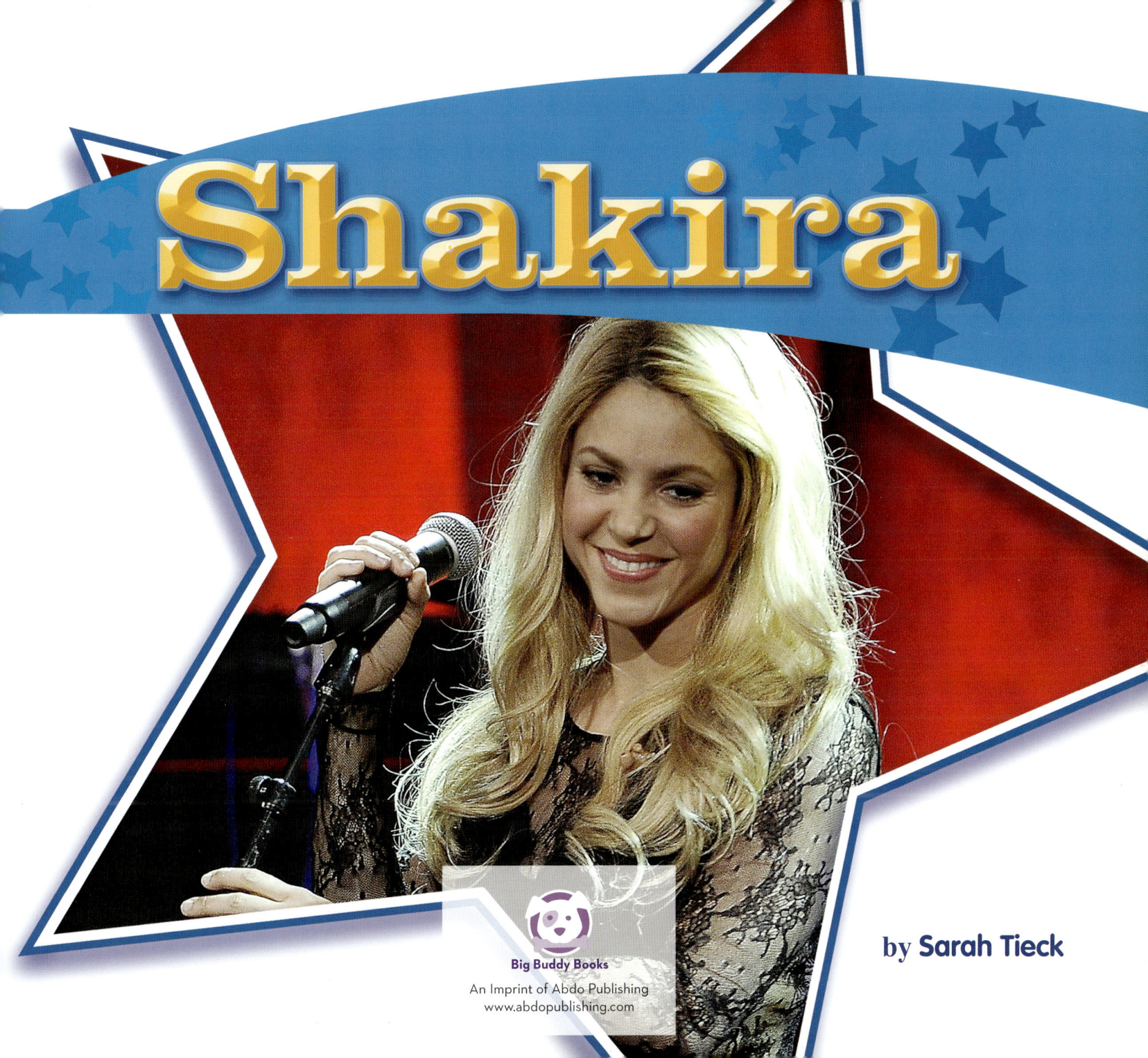

www.abdopublishing.com

Published by Abdo Publishing, a division of ABDO, PO Box 398166, Minneapolis, Minnesota 55439. Copyright © 2015 by Abdo Consulting Group, Inc. International copyrights reserved in all countries. No part of this book may be reproduced in any form without written permission from the publisher. Big Buddy Books™ is a trademark and logo of Abdo Publishing.

Printed in the United States of America, North Mankato, Minnesota.
092014
012015

Cover Photo: Chris Pizzello/Invision/AP.
Interior Photos: AFP/Getty Images (p. 13); ASSOCIATED PRESS (pp. 11, 15, 17, 19, 20, 21, 22); Getty Images (pp. 11, 27); ©iStockphoto.com (pp. 8, 11); Frank Micelotta/Invision/AP (p. 15); Chris Pizzello/Invision/AP (p. 28); Jordan Strauss/Invision/AP (p. 5); Charles Sykes/Invision/AP (p. 25); WireImage (p. 7).

Coordinating Series Editor: Rochelle Baltzer
Contributing Editors: Bridget O'Brien, Marcia Zappa
Graphic Design: Maria Hosley

Library of Congress Cataloging-in-Publication Data

Tieck, Sarah, 1976- author.
  Shakira : international music star / Sarah Tieck.
     pages cm. -- (Big buddy biographies)
  Audience: 7-11.
  ISBN 978-1-62403-573-9
 1. Shakira--Juvenile literature. 2. Singers--Latin America--Biography--Juvenile literature. I. Title.
  ML3930.S46T54 2015
  782.42164092--dc23
   [B]
                                           2014026440

Contents

Singing Star 4
Family Ties 6
Growing Up 9
Belly Dancer 10
Starting Out 12
New Opportunities 14
Big Break 18
The Voice 23
A Singer's Life 24
Off the Stage 26
Buzz 29
Snapshot 30
Important Words 31
Websites 31
Index 32

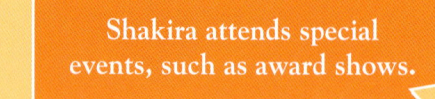
Shakira attends special events, such as award shows.

Singing Star

Shakira is a famous singer. She has won awards for her hit albums and songs. She also writes much of her music.

Shakira is especially known for her dancing. And, she is a **coach** on the popular television show *The Voice*.

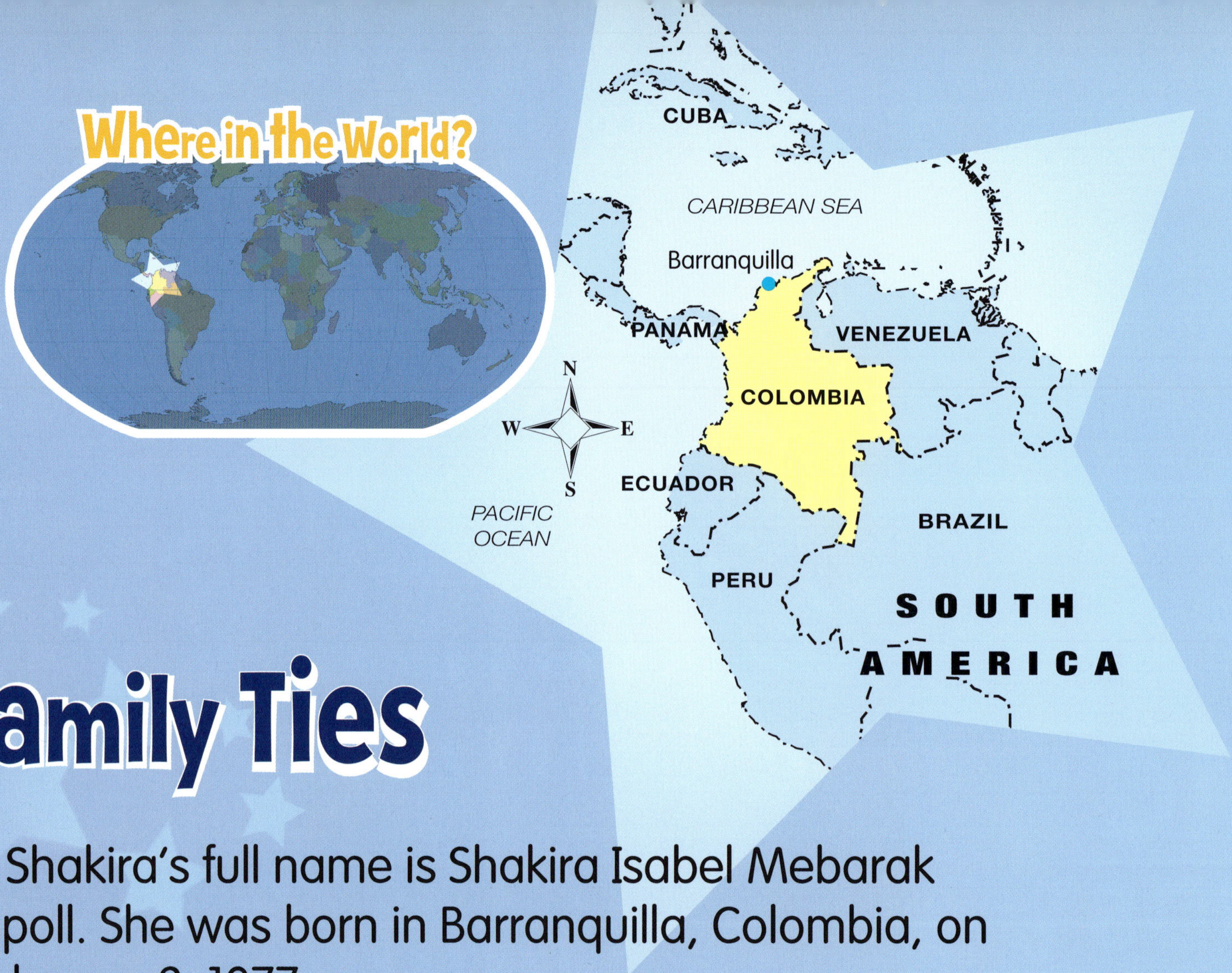

Where in the World?

Family Ties

Shakira's full name is Shakira Isabel Mebarak Ripoll. She was born in Barranquilla, Colombia, on February 2, 1977.

Shakira's parents are Nidia del Carmen Ripoll Torrado and William Mebarak Chadid. When Shakira was born, she had eight older half-siblings.

Shakira's father is Lebanese and her mother is Colombian.

Did you know...

Shakira's first song, "Tus Gafas Oscuras," was about her father's sunglasses.

Shakira grew up in Barranquilla. This city is near the Caribbean coast of Colombia.

Did you know...
Shakira had a sickness called smallpox when she was young. She still has a scar in the middle of her forehead from it.

Growing Up

As a child, Shakira came to love music and writing. She learned to write poems. Around age eight, she wrote her first song. By age ten, she was taking part in talent shows.

Young Shakira also discovered she loved dancing. And, she was naturally good at it.

Belly Dancer

Shakira enjoys belly dancing. This is a type of Middle Eastern dance. People move their hips and middles. Shakira uses belly dancing moves when she **performs** onstage.

Some people take lessons to learn belly dancing. But, Shakira taught herself. She came up with her own moves!

Shakira danced in the music video for "Hips Don't Lie."

In 2000, Shakira danced live at the Latin Grammy Awards.

Belly dancing costumes have beads that sparkle and jingle.

Did you know...
At age 13, Shakira moved to Bogota, Colombia, to be a model. Instead, she got a record contract!

Starting Out

Shakira worked hard. She enjoyed singing and dancing for others. By 1990, she had signed her first record contract.

In 1991, Shakira's first album came out. It is called *Magia*. In 1993, the album *Peligro* came out. For both albums, Shakira sang songs in Spanish. Neither had strong sales. But, Shakira was excited to have a start.

Shakira's style was different in 1999, when she was early in her career.

New Opportunities

After her first two albums, Shakira took a break to act on the Colombian **soap opera** *El Oasis*. She spent time listening to other singers. In 1995, she began recording rock and **pop** songs.

In 1996, *Pies Descalzos* came out. It was Shakira's first international album. It sold 5 million copies. Soon, Shakira moved to the United States.

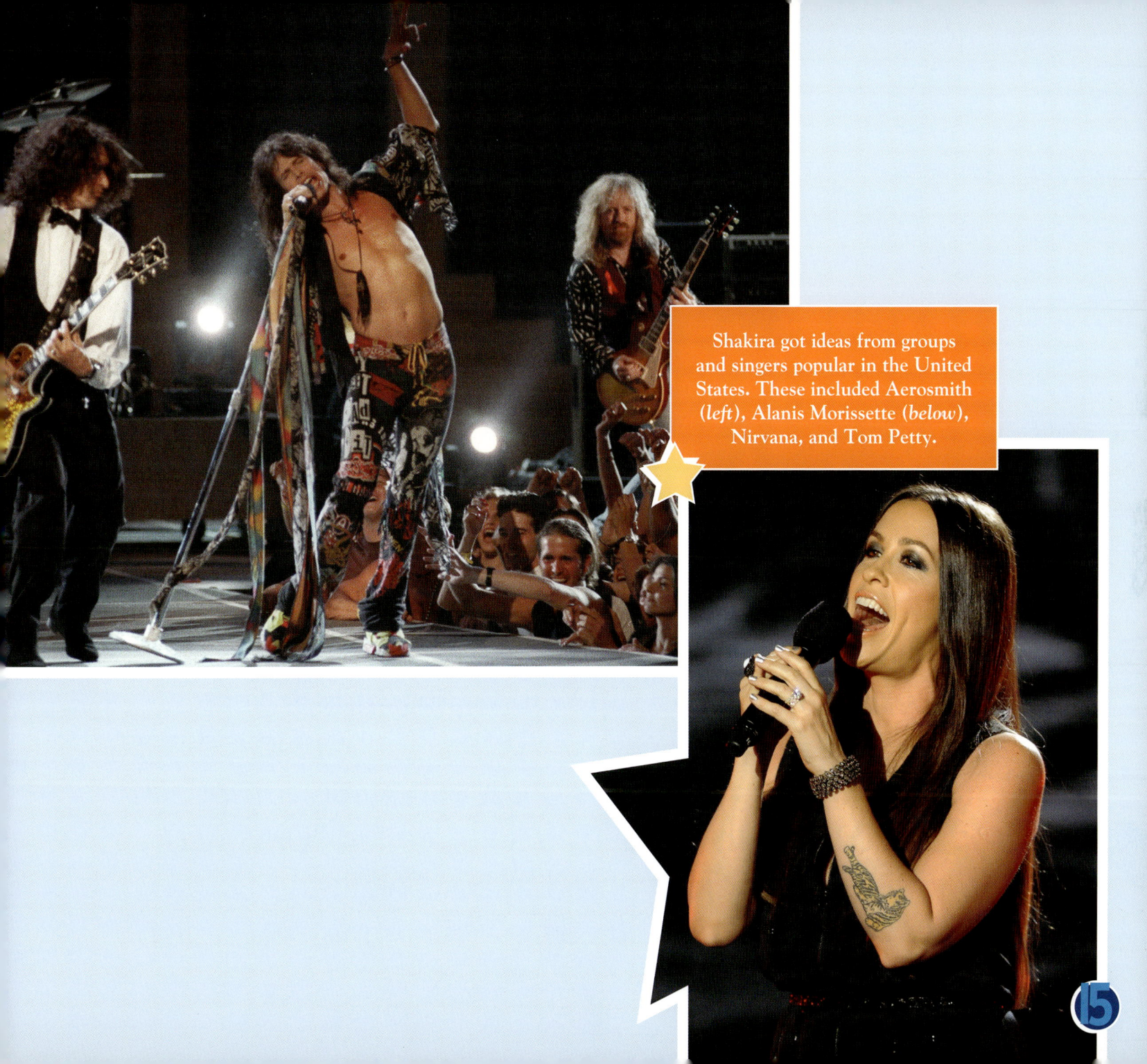

Shakira got ideas from groups and singers popular in the United States. These included Aerosmith (*left*), Alanis Morissette (*below*), Nirvana, and Tom Petty.

In 1998, Shakira came out with a new album. It is called *¿Dónde Están Los Ladrones?* People loved her **pop** and rock songs. Shakira grew especially famous in Europe and Latin America for a song called "Ojos Así."

Despite this, Shakira wanted to be a hit in the United States. So, she began learning to write songs in English.

In 2000, *Shakira: MTV Unplugged* came out. It was a hit! It earned Shakira a Grammy Award for Best Latin Pop Album.

> **Did you know...**
> Shakira has danced and sang in Pepsi commercials.

Big Break

In 2001, Shakira's first English language album came out. It is called *Laundry Service*. "Whenever, Wherever" was its first hit song. The album sold more than 13 million copies!

Shakira's 2005 album had two parts. The first was in Spanish. The second was in English. Shakira won awards for her work. She went on tour to **perform** and **promote** her music.

In 2006, Shakira's song "Hips Don't Lie" came out. She performed with Wyclef Jean (*right*).

In 2009, Shakira **released** the album *She Wolf*. "She Wolf" was one of its hit songs.

Shakira put out *Sale El Sol* in 2010. She also sang a song for the 2010 FIFA World Cup. It was called "Waka Waka (This Time for Africa)." Many people watched the music video on YouTube.

Shakira traveled to South Africa for the World Cup. She spent time meeting kids and teaching them to dance.

Shakira performed near the end of the World Cup.

Adam Levine, Shakira, Usher, and Blake Shelton (*left to right*) were judges on *The Voice* in 2013.

The Voice

In 2013, Shakira appeared as a judge and **coach** on *The Voice*. This television show finds talented singers.

Shakira and three other judges chose the finalists. This took Shakira's work and talents in a new direction.

A Singer's Life

Shakira spends time working on her songs and **performances**. She goes to recording **studios** to make albums. She also **produces** her albums.

Shakira works hard to **promote** her albums and *The Voice*. She appears on television and in magazines. And, she practices and performs live for fans.

Fans often take pictures with Shakira.

Did you know...

Shakira's partner is Gerard Piqué. He is a famous soccer player in Barcelona! Shakira and Gerard have a son named Milan.

Off the Stage

Shakira spends free time with her family. They live in Barcelona, Spain. They also spend time in the United States. They enjoy being active and traveling.

Shakira likes to help others. She started the Barefoot Foundation in 1997. This group helps children in Colombia get an education.

Shakira is a UNICEF goodwill ambassador. She travels the world to help children in need.

Shakira performed at the 2014 Billboard Music Awards.

Buzz

Shakira's album *Shakira* came out in 2014. One of its first hit songs was "Can't Remember to Forget You." Also that year, Shakira returned as a judge and **coach** on *The Voice*. Fans are excited for more music from Shakira!

Snapshot

⭐ **Name**: Shakira Isabel Mebarak Ripoll

⭐ **Birthday**: February 2, 1977

⭐ **Birthplace**: Barranquilla, Colombia

⭐ **Albums**: Magia, Peligro, Pies Descalzos, ¿Dónde Están Los Ladrones?, Shakira: MTV Unplugged, Laundry Service, She Wolf, Sale El Sol, Shakira

⭐ **Appearances**: El Oasis, The Voice

Important Words

coach someone who teaches or trains a person or a group on a certain subject or skill.

perform to do something in front of an audience. A performance is the act of doing something, such as singing or acting, in front of an audience.

pop relating to popular music.

produce to oversee the making of a movie, a play, an album, or a radio or television show.

promote to help something become known.

release to make available to the public.

soap opera a television show that has continuing stories about the daily lives and problems of a group of characters.

studio a place where music is recorded.

Websites

To learn more about Big Buddy Biographies, visit **booklinks.abdopublishing.com**. These links are routinely monitored and updated to provide the most current information available.

Index

Aerosmith **15**

awards **4, 17, 18**

Barefoot Foundation **26**

belly dancing **10, 11**

charity work **26, 27**

Colombia **6, 7, 8, 12, 14, 26, 30**

¿Dónde Están Los Ladrones? (album) **16, 30**

El Oasis (television show) **14, 30**

family **6, 7, 26**

Jean, Wyclef **19**

Laundry Service (album) **18, 30**

Levine, Adam **22**

Magia (album) **12, 30**

Morissette, Alanis **15**

Nirvana **15**

Peligro (album) **12, 30**

Petty, Tom **15**

Pies Descalzos (album) **14, 30**

Piqué, Gerard **26**

Sale El Sol (album) **20, 30**

Shakira (album) **29, 30**

Shakira: MTV Unplugged (album) **17, 30**

She Wolf (album) **20, 30**

Shelton, Blake **22**

Spain **26**

UNICEF **27**

United States **14, 15, 16, 26**

Usher **22**

Voice, The (television show) **4, 22, 23, 24, 29, 30**